MY FIRST CHRISTMAS

High Contrast Baby Book

THIS BOOK BELONGS TO:

GUIDANCES

HOW OFTEN SHOULD YOU VIEW THE BOOKS?

Do it every day. Show your child for at least a few minutes every day. "Watch as much as you can."

HOW LONG SHOULD CHILDREN LOOK AT BLACK AND WHITE CARDS?

Let your child focus on the picture for a short time, no longer than 30 seconds at a time.

MOTOR DEVELOPMENT - HAND-EYE?

Encourage your child to reach for the card and examine it with their hands.

HO-HO-HO!

HERE IS YOUR GIFT:
https://bit.ly/4f4YOoW

**TAP THIS LINK IN THE BROWSER AND ENJOY!
IF YOU LOVED THE BOOK AND THE GIFT GIVE US**

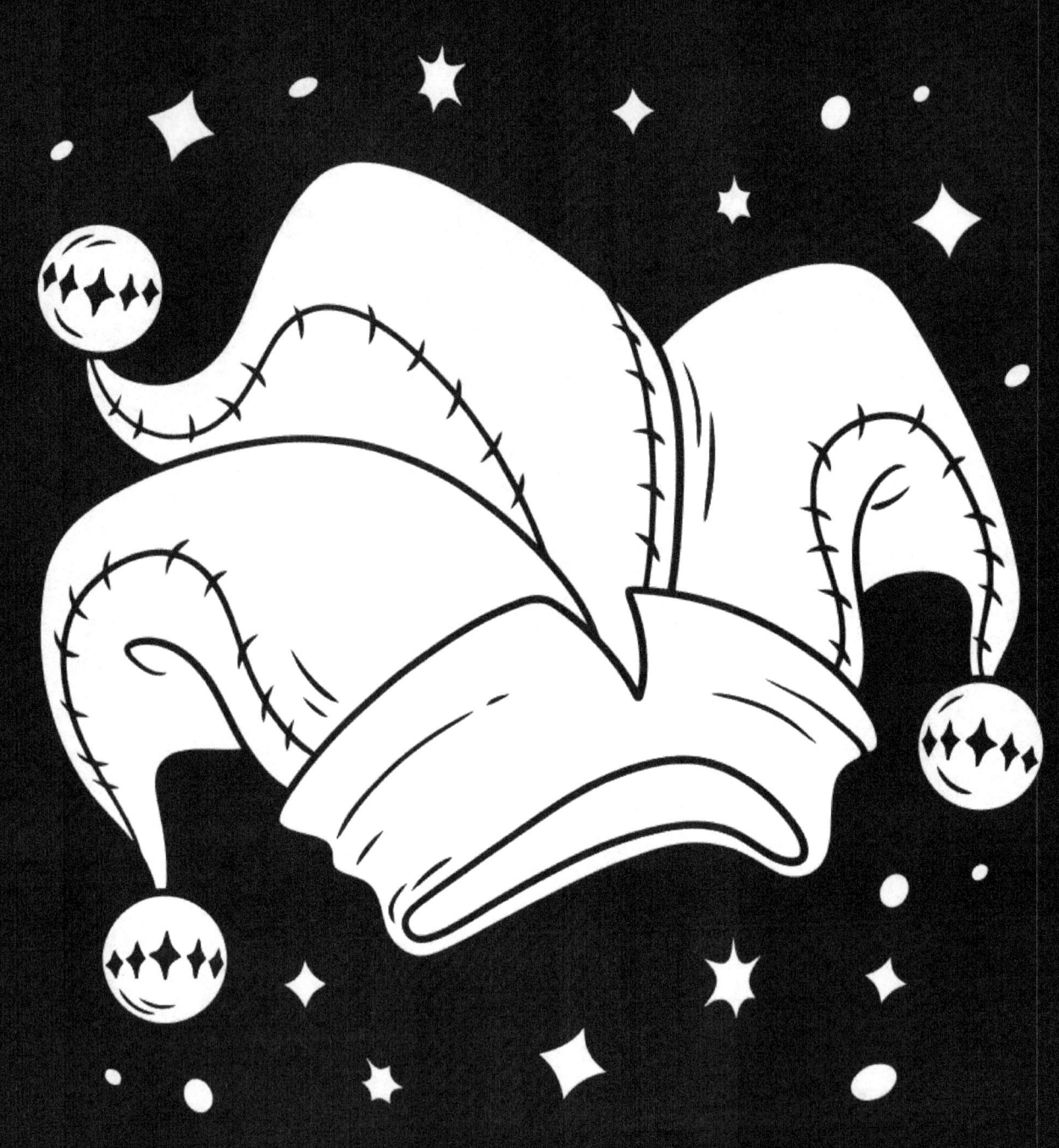

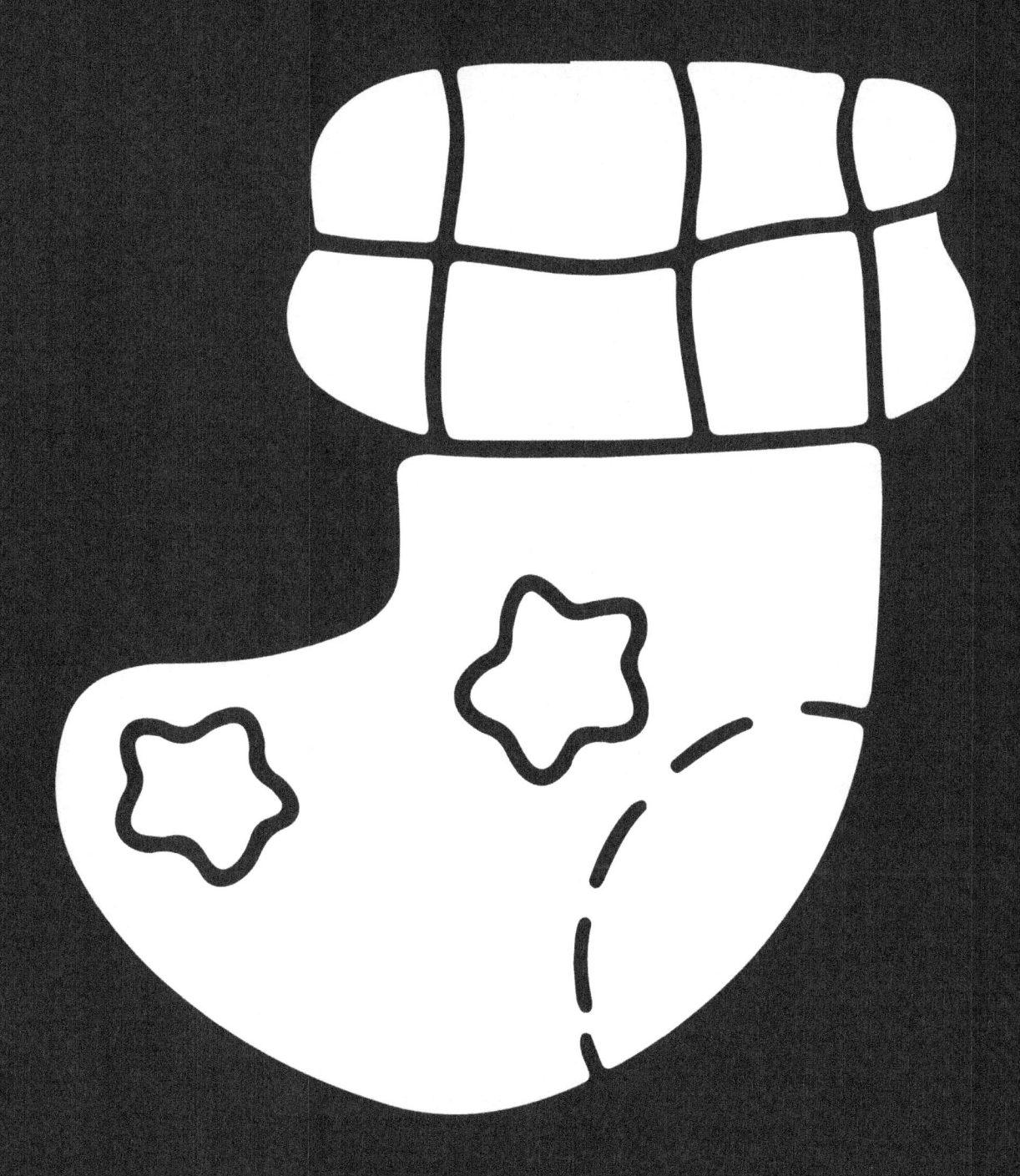

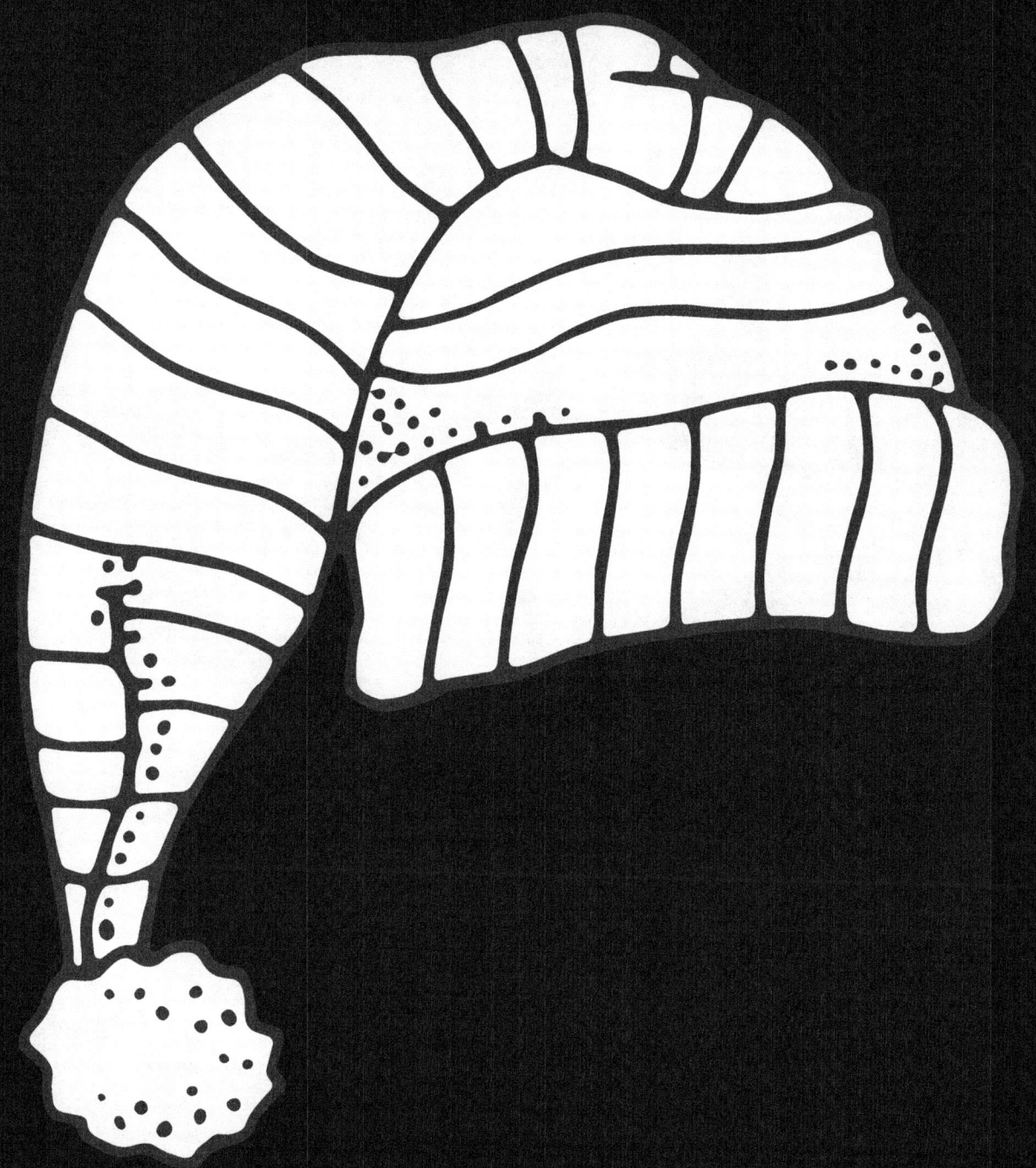

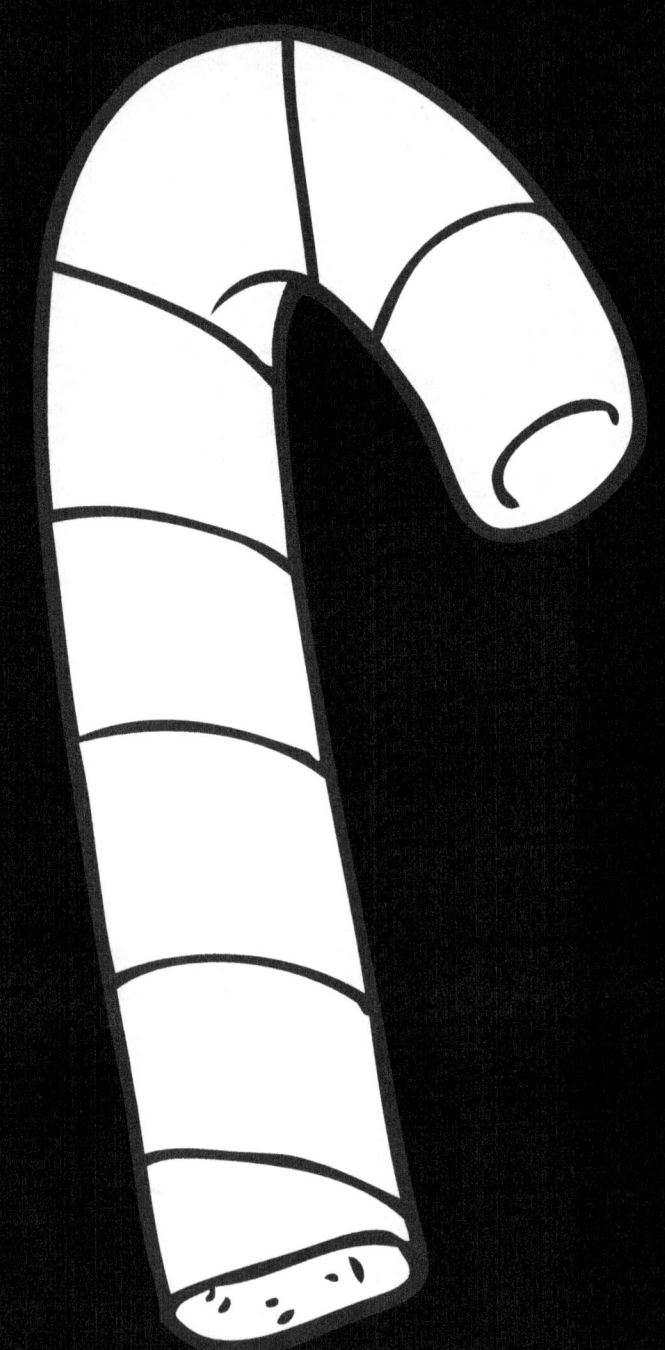

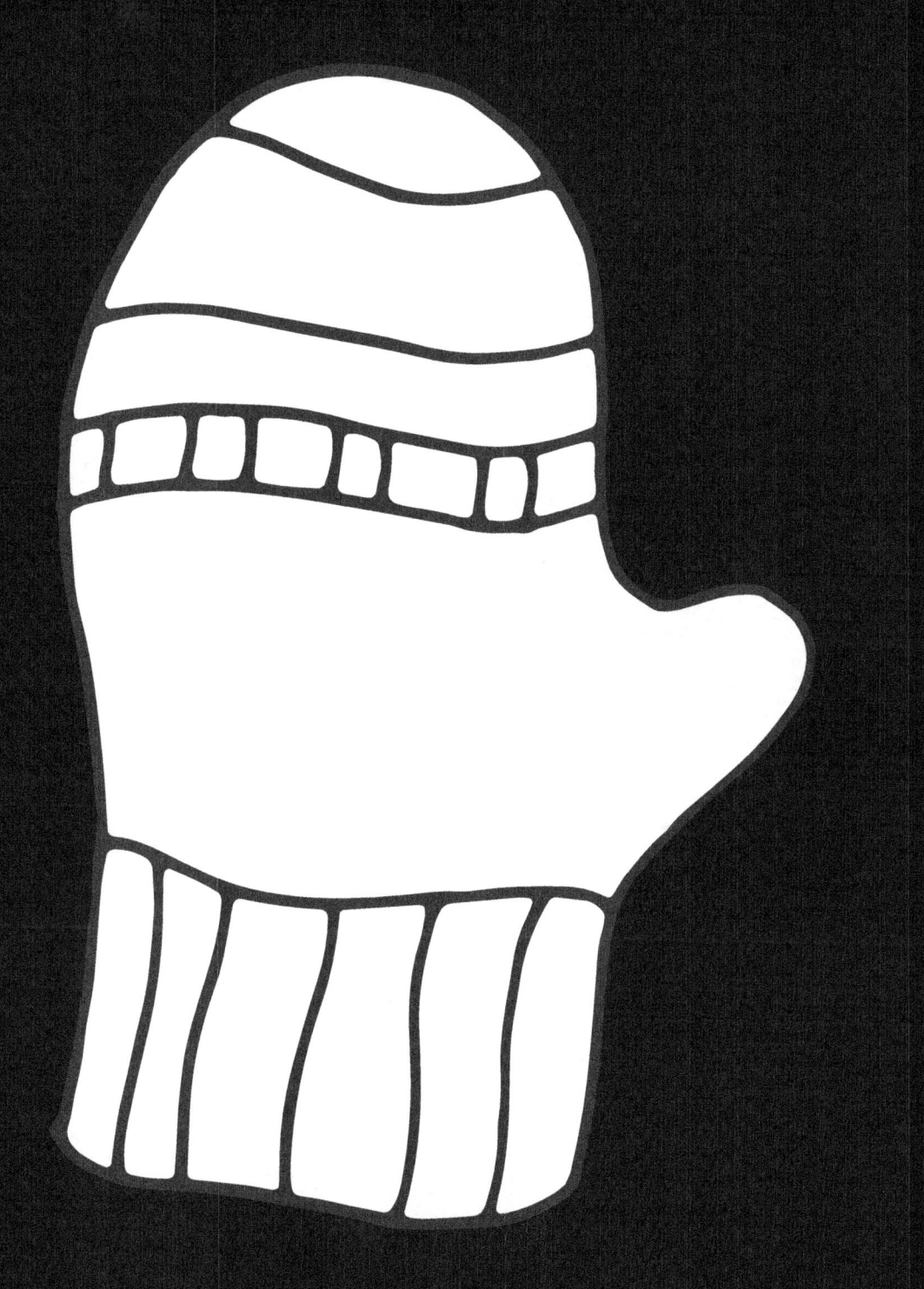

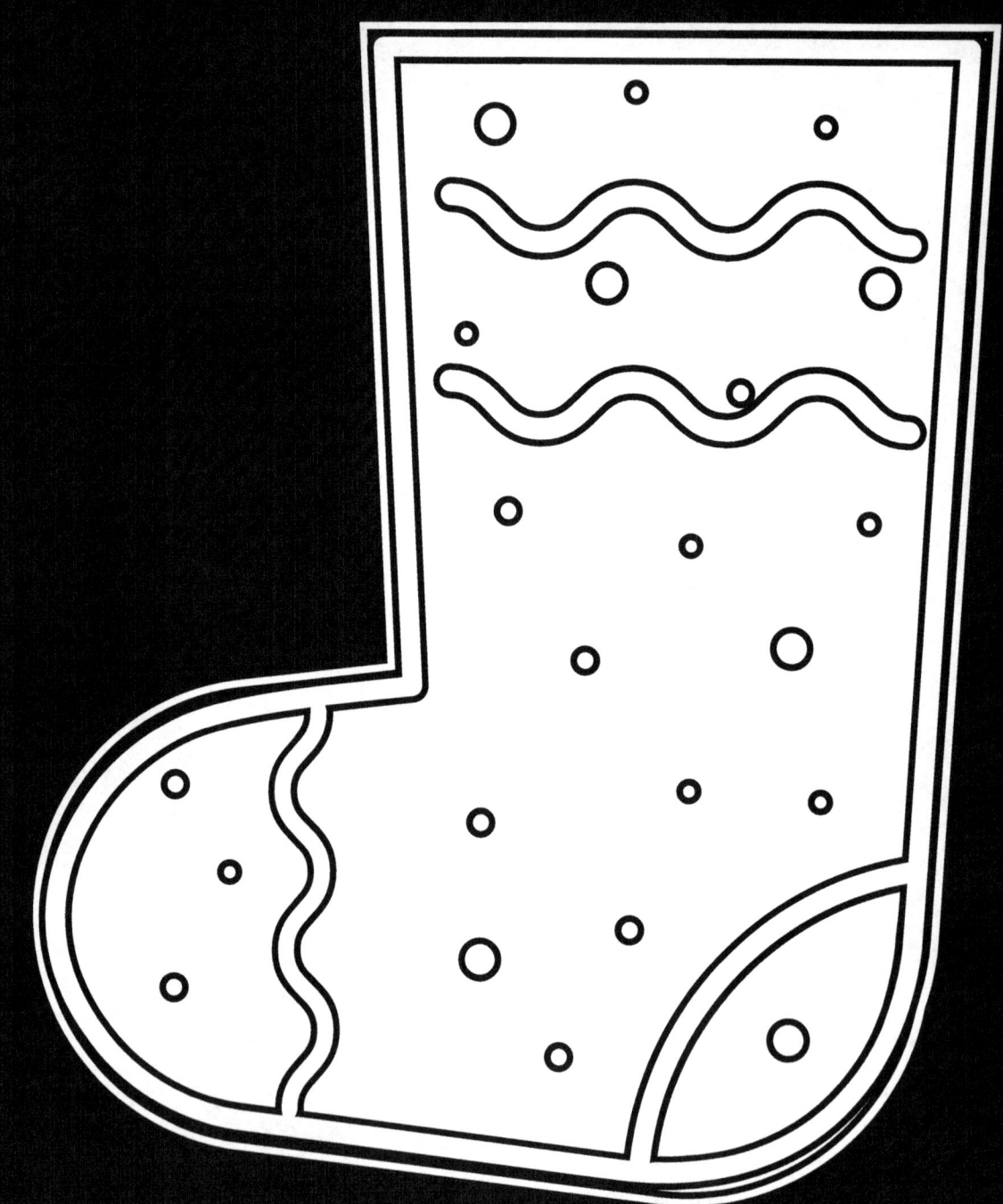

Printed in Dunstable, United Kingdom